...o and Organ Accompaniment

Great Hymns

Instrumental Solos for Worship

Available books

Flute, Oboe, Violin - CMP 0354-00-400
B♭ Clarinet, B♭ Tenor Saxophone - CMP 0355-00-400
E♭ Alto Saxophone - CMP 0356-00-400
B♭ Trumpet - CMP 0357-00-400
Trombone, Euphonium BC/TC - CMP 0358-00-400
F Horn/E♭ Horn - CMP 0351-00-400

CURNOW®
MUSIC

EXCLUSIVELY DISTRIBUTED BY

HAL•LEONARD®
CORPORATION

7777 W. BLUEMOUND RD. P.O. BOX 13819 MILWAUKEE, WI 53213

Arranged by James Curnow

Order number: CMP 0359-00-401

James Curnow
Great Hymns
Piano and Organ Accompaniment

ISBN 978-90-431-0983-3
NUGI 443

Printed in Holland.

Great Hymns

Instrumental Solos for Worship

Contents

INTRODUCTION

This collection of some of the world's greatest hymns was created for, and is dedicated to, my good friend and musical colleague, Philip Smith, Principal Trumpet, New York Philharmonic Orchestra. The goal of these arrangements is to allow instrumentalists the opportunity to give praise and adoration to God through their musical abilities.

Though the arrangements have been written for trumpet, with Phil in mind, cued notes have been added to allow players at many different levels and on various instruments to perform them. They are also playable on all instruments (C treble clef, Bb Treble Clef, Eb, F or Bass Clef) by simply purchasing the appropriate book that coincides with the key of their instrument.

The piano accompaniment book has been written to work with all instruments or an accompaniment track for each hymn is included on the compact disc, should a piano accompanist not be available. Appropriate tuning notes have also been added to the compact disc recording to allow the soloists the opportunity to adjust their intonation to the intonation of the compact disc accompaniment.

May you enjoy using this collection and find it useful in extending your musical ministry.

Kindest regards,

James Curnow
President
Curnow Music Press, Inc.

Dedicated to Philip Smith, Principal Trumpet, New York Philharmonic Orchestra

ALL CREATURES OF OUR GOD AND KING

Lasst Uns Erfreuen

Arr. **James Curnow** (ASCAP)

Dedicated to Philip Smith, Principal Trumpet, New York Philharmonic Orchestra

PRAISE TO THE LORD, THE ALMIGHTY

Lobe Den Herren

Arr. **James Curnow** (ASCAP)

Dedicated to Philip Smith, Principal Trumpet, New York Philharmonic Orchestra

BE THOU MY VISION
Slane

Arr. **James Curnow** (ASCAP)

Dedicated to Philip Smith, Principal Trumpet, New York Philharmonic Orchestra

O WORSHIP THE KING
Lyons

Arr. **James Curnow** (ASCAP)

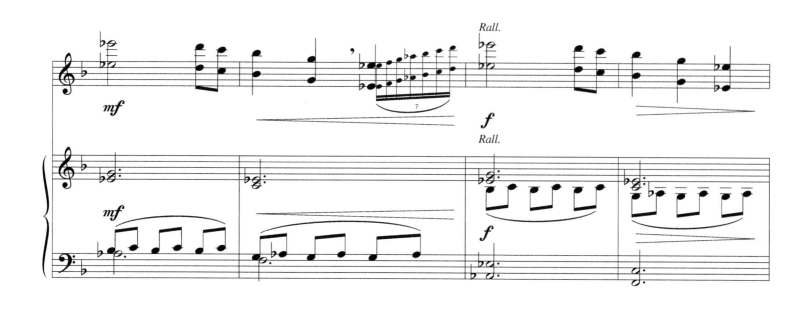

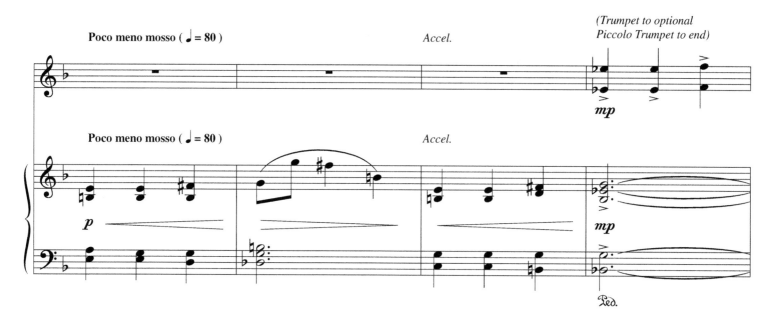

Dedicated to Philip Smith, Principal Trumpet, New York Philharmonic Orchestra

JOYFUL, JOYFUL, WE ADORE THEE

Hymn to Joy

Arr. **James Curnow** (ASCAP)

22

Dedicated to Philip Smith, Principal Trumpet, New York Philharmonic Orchestra

BRETHREN, WE HAVE MET TO WORSHIP

Holy Manna Variations

Arr. **James Curnow** (ASCAP)

28

Dedicated to Philip Smith, Principal Trumpet, New York Philharmonic Orchestra

WE GATHER TOGETHER

Kremser

Arr. **James Curnow** (ASCAP)

Dedicated to Philip Smith, Principal Trumpet, New York Philharmonic Orchestra

I SING THE MIGHTY POWER OF GOD

Ellacombe

Arr. **James Curnow** (ASCAP)

Dedicated to Philip Smith, Principal Trumpet, New York Philharmonic Orchestra

A MIGHTY FORTRESS IS OUR GOD

Ein' Feste Burg

Arr. **James Curnow** (ASCAP)

Dedicated to Philip Smith, Principal Trumpet, New York Philharmonic Orchestra

ALL HAIL THE POWER

Coronation, Diadem, Miles Lane

Arr. **James Curnow** (ASCAP)

Piano and Organ Accompaniment